Original title:
Through the Garden Gate

Copyright © 2025 Creative Arts Management OÜ
All rights reserved.

Author: Elliot Harrison
ISBN HARDBACK: 978-1-80567-034-6
ISBN PAPERBACK: 978-1-80567-114-5

## The Allure of the Plot

In the yard where gnomes all prance,
A squirrel does his silly dance.
With acorns tossed by zealous hands,
He scampers round like he owns the lands.

The roses giggle, the daisies tease,
A bee buzzes by with greatest ease.
He steals a sip, then bumps his head,
And tumbles down to the flower bed.

The fence is low, the weeds are tall,
A rabbit hops, and we all fall.
He snatches carrots from right under,
Then darts away like a silent thunder.

A snail in shell, so slow and grand,
Claims the path like it's his own land.
With every inch, a quest so bold,
He'll win the race—if time's on hold!

## The Silent Butterfly

A butterfly flutters, oh so bold,
It chooses paths not easily told.
In a dance with the breeze, it takes a spin,
Then lands on my nose, where do I begin?

It giggles and tickles, can't keep its place,
With each little laugh, it just wants some space.
I flail like a dancer, all arms and despair,
It flaps its wings, and I'm gasping for air!

## **Blooming Memories**

In the garden, flowers shout with glee,
Petunias gossip, as bright as can be.
They reminisce 'bout the bees they knew,
Who buzzed their names under skies so blue.

Then comes a worm in a stylish hat,
Claiming he's quite the acrobat.
He flips and flops, what a daring feat,
But all of his moves end in a seat!

## A Tapestry of Vines

Vines twist and twirl like a circus crew,
Tangled in tales, what mischief they brew.
They rope in the sun, a professor's friend,
But they get caught, and it's all on the mend!

With leaves a-chatter, they share bold views,
On the latest trends in the garden news.
A frog in a top hat hops by with style,
Declaring each bloom makes the critics smile!

## **Lanterns in the Twilight**


As twilight falls, the lanterns sway,
Fireflies join, in a curious play.
They flicker and flash, giving whispers bright,
But one little bug thinks it's too much light!

He spins in a circle, then darts with a zoom,
Collides with a flower, creating a boom!
The flower chuckles, "You've got some nerve!"
As he grumbles away, it's what he deserves!

# A Window to Earth's Heart

In the sun, the daisies chat,
Chattering away, just like a cat.
Bees wear tiny hats, they claim,
Buzzing about in this wacky game.

A worm reads poetry, slithers near,
Its book is soggy, but it has no fear.
Rabbits gossip over a patch of greens,
Sharing tales of what's fit for beans.

The old oak tree taps its roots,
Complaining of bugs in its shiny boots.
Squirrels perform acrobatics bold,
Proving that laughter never gets old.

## The Enchanted Bower Awaiting

Under skies so dreamy bright,
A frog sings opera, what a sight!
But who'd believe a croak could charm,
It's just a show; there's no real harm.

Ladybugs wear polka-dot ties,
Flying around with fashionable sighs.
They gossip with butterflies, oh so grand,
Trading secrets from flower to land.

In the air, a canvas of colors bends,
While the sun drips honey, and laughter lends.
Every leaf rolls like a comedy reel,
In this sweet spot, joy is the feel.

## Seasons Unfolding Underfoot

Spring sneezes, and flowers bloom,
While winter grumbles in the room.
Summertime jokes flow like a stream,
Chasing all shadows, it's a wild dream.

Autumn scatters leaves like confetti,
Bragging about colors—oh so pretty!
Squirrels hoard snacks for a dark day,
While the pumpkins wink in their orange play.

Each step we take on this playful ground,
Echoes with giggles that swirl around.
With each season, a new jest unfolds,
A comedy of life that never gets old.

## The Call of Fluttering Wings


Birds in bow ties pirouette and dance,
Flapping their wings as if in a trance.
They hold a concert at the break of dawn,
While the sun yawns, stretching its brawn.

A parrot with flair recites a pun,
Each joke a jet stream: oh, what fun!
The pigeons roll their eyes in dismay,
"Not another feathered cabaret!"

Fluffy clouds giggle, making shapes,
As butterflies sketch their playful drapes.
In the meadow's arms, laughter rings,
Delighting all with their flappy flings.

## Secrets of the Trellis

There's a squirrel in the roses,
Wearing shades and a hat.
He's planning a big heist,
For some snacks on a mat.

A gopher with a monocle,
Studying the lawn.
He charts all the tunnels,
For his party at dawn.

Bees gossip in circles,
Trading sweet, sticky tales.
With laughter and buzzing,
They hail the flower trails.

The hedgehog is a poet,
Reciting under a tree.
His verses are prickly,
But his charm is quite free.

## The Essence of Twilight

As twilight whispers softly,
The crickets start their play.
A frog sings off-key loudly,
While the moon starts to sway.

Mice throw a wild dance party,
With crumbs from yesterday's feast.
A snail is the DJ,
Spinning tracks from the east.

Fireflies flash their secrets,
In a dance of pure delight.
They shimmer like confetti,
In the warm summer night.

A raccoon hosts a pizza night,
With toppings of pure fun.
He juggles slices clumsily,
'Til they drop one by one.

## Moments in the Mulberry

The mulberry's ripe and wobbly,
With berries that love to burst.
A grand feast for the birds,
Who nibble to quench their thirst.

A hedgehog rolls in laughter,
As a berry foes fly.
They stick to his little snout,
As he grins at the sky.

Squirrels start up a rumor,
That this tree has a prize.
An acorn crown for the bold,
Who can reach for the skies.

Pigeons gossip in the branches,
Spreading tales with a coo.
They claim the fruit holds magic,
And it's good for a stew.

# Faces of the Fruit Tree

The apple tree wears glasses,
With leaves that look so wise.
It watches squirrels scramble,
In their nut-gathering ties.

The pear tree sings in laughter,
Its branches swaying wide.
It's quite the smooth talker,
With no reason to hide.

Cherries giggle at secrets,
They dangle from the vine.
With every little breeze,
They dance like they're divine.

Plums pull funny faces,
As they ripen in the sun.
They know they'll be a treat,
When dinner time is done.

## Pathways to the Unknown

A ladybug lost on a stroll,
Chasing a frog with a roll,
They giggle and hop under sun,
Creating mischief, oh what fun!

The hedgehogs play hide-and-seek,
With prickles, it's quite a cheek!
They dart and laugh behind the trees,
Sharing secrets with buzzing bees.

A rabbit tied up in a knot,
Thinks he's clever, but he's not.
He wiggles and wriggles, what a sight!
Dance, bunny, under moonlight.

Through daisies, ants march, so proud,
Forming a line, they're so loud.
They trip on petals, their parade,
A funny scene this garden made.

## A Symphony of Petals

In a meadow of colors bold,
Tiny flowers sing, or so I'm told.
With each breeze, they shake and quiver,
A melody that makes you shiver.

A sunflower with a great big grin,
Spills secrets of thrum and spin.
It tips its hat to a blushing rose,
As bumblebees buzz by with their prose.

I found a peacock taking a nap,
Nestled snug in a green grass lap.
It dreams of feathers, flying high,
Wakes up confused, thinking he's shy.

The wind whirls, tickling each bloom,
Creating an uproar, a floral boom.
Petals scatter, laughter takes flight,
In this silly garden, what a delight!

## The Hidden Blooms

Behind the fence, where no one goes,
Lies a place where the wild thyme grows.
With mushrooms dancing, hats so tall,
They invite the pixies to a ball.

A toadstool chef cooks up a stew,
Using rain droplets and grass for a brew.
He spills it all with a cackle and cheer,
While squirrels gather, filling with fear.

A sneaky snail in a racing sport,
Claims he's the fastest, what a retort!
He slides by slow while boasting so grand,
And leaves behind a slimy strand.

The daisies gossip, whisper so light,
They chuckle as butterflies take flight.
In this hidden spot, where the odd ones play,
The world's a stage in a magical way.

## **Enchanted Flora**

In a patch where carrots wear hats,
And cabbage strums tunes with cats.
Each vine sings softly, a playful tune,
Beneath the gaze of a chuckling moon.

A parakeet pretends to be wise,
Teaching the daisies to leap and rise.
"Jump higher!" it squawks with a feathery glee,
While tumbling tulips join in for free.

Bumblebees play chess on a leaf,
Gathering honey, seeking relief.
They bicker and buzz, each thinking they're right,
In this garden tale, what a sight!

The petunias paint with colors proud,
Tickling each other, laughing loud.
In this enchanted space of pure jest,
The garden blooms, and we're all guests.

## **The Intimacy of Thorns**

In a patch where the roses grow,
Entwined with prickles in a row.
I tiptoe past, a cautious glance,
Afraid to lose my pants in trance.

The daisies laugh, their heads held high,
While thorns conspire, oh my, oh my!
A garden meeting gone askew,
With prickly hugs that leave a bruise.

A bumblebee in ruffled flight,
Stung by petals, what a sight!
He shouts, "I swear I'm not a fool!"
In this circus, humor's the rule.

Yet under all the thorny fuss,
A twinkle hides amongst the rust.
Among this chaos, fun can't wait,
Just watch your step, and guard your gait.

## Pools of Light and Shadow

In puddles where the sunlight plays,
The butterflies dance in their ways.
A shadow lurks, but don't be scared,
It's just a rabbit, slightly impaired.

With every hop, he seems to glide,
But trips on grass like he's untied.
The sunbeams giggle, they can't help,
As flowers quiver, stifling yelp.

At dusk the glowworms sketch their art,
While crickets play the violins' part.
A symphony of nature's cheer,
Making shadows feel more dear.

So here we sit, on mossy stones,
With laughter echoing in tones.
These pools reflect both dark and bright,
In gardening fun, we find delight!

## Fables of the Frangipani

Under frangipani's fragrant charm,
Sits a squirrel, intent to disarm.
With acorns stashed, he schemes and plots,
A nutty heist with tangled knots.

Blossoms blush in the sunny breeze,
While ants march forth, intent to tease.
They wave their tiny limbs with glee,
Causing chaos among the tree.

A tortoise wobbles, slow and grand,
Feigning wisdom, takes a stand.
"Don't rush!" he shouts with quiet zest,
As nimble critters pass the test.

In this realm where follies play,
Each fragrance whispers, "Stay, oh stay!"
For in the tales the flowers weave,
A laugh is what we all believe.

## The Dance of Dewdrops

When morning breaks with sparkling grace,
Dewdrops shimmer on every face.
They jiggle past, so light and spry,
Just try to catch them—oh my, oh my!

A ladybug with legs so short,
Goes waltzing by—oh, what a sport!
She trips and twirls, then gives a laugh,
In this ball, she's the epitaph.

The daisies clap, their petals wide,
As raindrops join this joyful ride.
With giggles shared among the grass,
In nature's ball, no time to pass.

So tip your hat, and join the fun,
With every drop, the day's begun.
In tiny worlds where laughter's sown,
We find delight, we're never alone.

## Sanctuary of Scented Euphoria

In the realm where flowers giggle,
Bees wear tiny helmets, all a wiggle.
Daisies play hide and seek in flair,
While butterflies dance without a care.

Laughter wafts on the breeze like wine,
Petunias gossip, their petals entwine.
A daffodil tells a joke so sly,
While sunflowers wink and birds just fly.

**Promises Hidden in Thorns**

Roses flaunt their beauty with pride,
Yet lurk the thorns where secrets reside.
A cheeky briar whispers to the breeze,
'Though I'm prickly, do come, if you please!'

Cacti wearing hats chuckle in style,
While ivy vines stretch, looking versatile.
With laughter lurking in every bloom,
Even nature can't resist the room.

## The Flutter of Petals in Flight

Petals pirouette, a floral ballet,
As bees form a band, sweet music to play.
Geraniums gossip about daisies' charm,
While lilacs giggle, causing alarm.

A wind chime made of leaves starts to clink,
Creating a melody in nature's wink.
Hummingbirds hum along, just for fun,
In this garden stage, where all things run.

## Varieties of Serenity Unveiled

In a patchwork quilt of colors bright,
Sunlight spills laughter, a pure delight.
Lavender winks, its fragrance so sweet,
While pansies put on a show with their feet.

The weeds roll their eyes, just trying to chill,
While daisies craft dreams in the soft, green hill.
A frog in the pond, with a top hat and cane,
Croaks out a tune, oh, the joy, so insane!

## Echoes of the Meadow

In a field where daisies dance,
A chicken fell, forgot its prance.
The rabbits giggle, shake their heads,
While ants conspire in tiny beds.

A frog in specs, he reads a book,
A wild hare wanders, takes a look.
The blushing tulips tease the bees,
A snail contests with every breeze.

Squirrels play tag on tipsy boughs,
A butterfly won't share its vows.
The meadow's laughter fills the air,
As nature's jesters entertain with flair.

With every rustle, joy expands,
In this quirky land of broken plans.
The sun winks down, a cosmic jester,
Chasing shadows, our mighty tester.

## The Old Wisteria Arch

Beneath the arch where shadows cling,
A cat debates if life's a fling.
With lazy paws it swipes a fly,
As giggling children loiter by.

The blossoms whisper secret jokes,
While squirrels tease the nesting folks.
A mad hat mouse decides to bake,
And serves up cheese that starts to quake.

The old dog snores, a barky dream,
As birds unite, a feathery team.
A squirrel's prank earns laughter loud,
As petals float, they form a cloud.

Through blooms adorned with purple hues,
We find a world of funny views.
This arch a portal to delight,
Where whimsy reigns both day and night.

## Raindrops on Sunlit Leaves

Beneath the leaves, a chorus sings,
Of raindrops falling, bouncing things.
A worm wears boots, slips with a grin,
While puddles form a dance within.

The startled frog leaps, can't be late,
For all the fun that raindrops create.
The flowers giggle, splash and sway,
As muddy piglets join the fray.

A parrot swipes a paper hat,
While squirrels plot a pitter-pat.
The sun peeks out, a cheeky grin,
As laughter bubbles from within.

Each droplet tells a funny tale,
Of clumsy critters on a trail.
Across the garden, joy unfolds,
In every raindrop, laughter holds.

## Shadows of the Sunflower

Sunflowers stretch to catch the rays,
While shadows fall in funny ways.
A turtle waits, a sunlight tease,
Sneaking up on drowsy bees.

The petals giggle, whisper low,
As grasshoppers put on a show.
A beetle's dance, it trips and spins,
As flowers cheer with capered grins.

The sunbeam slides, the light has fun,
While all around, the critters run.
A lazy lizard, sunbathing bold,
Cracks a joke that's centuries old.

Through shadowed paths of golden glow,
Each moment's filled with laughter's flow.
In this garden, silly and bright,
The sunflowers laugh, igniting light.

## Beneath the Boughs

Beneath the boughs, the squirrels play,
Chasing shadows in a silly way.
A hedgehog sneezes, rolls in surprise,
While birds perform their acrobatic flies.

A rabbit hops, with ears in the air,
Munching on carrots without a care.
The flowers giggle, swaying in breeze,
As bees discuss their honey with ease.

Crickets chirp a tune quite absurd,
While ants debate what's best in the world.
Laughter echoes from tree to tree,
In this madcap land of whimsy and glee.

## The Garden's Caress

The tulips gossip, they can't be shy,
While daisies laugh at butterflies that fly.
A cucumber floats, just like a boat,
While peas engage in a playful note.

The sun peeks down, a curious king,
As ladybugs dance, each with a fling.
A radical worm writes poems in dirt,
Declaring love for snails in their skirt.

With jokes so corny, even the corn laughs,
And pumpkins tell tales of their silly paths.
In this patch of joy, what a surprise,
A garden alive, where humor lies!

## Seasonal Reverie

In spring, the blooms tell tales of jest,
While butterflies wear polka dots, dressed best.
A daffodil cracks jokes with a rose,
As raindrops giggle, how funny it goes.

Summer swings with bees in a dance,
With flowers in hats, they take a chance.
The sun's a clown, with rays that tease,
Inviting clouds for a ticklish breeze.

Autumn chuckles with crunching leaves,
While pumpkins don faces, no tricks up sleeves.
The air is filled with a caramel scent,
As laughter and cheer in colors are pent.

# Petal-Laden Pathways

On petal-laden paths, the fun begins,
Where laughter spins like a whirly-wins.
A gnome tells stories, goofy and grand,
While fairies play marbles in the sand.

Cabbages gossip as they burst out loud,
While shadows prance, all merry and proud.
The sun ducks low, a jester so bright,
And plays hide and seek with the approaching night.

The lilies make crowns for all who pass,
Creating a fashion from blades of grass.
Each step brings joy, a silly delight,
In this whimsical garden full of light!

**Entrance to Reverie**

In a land where gnomes dance,
And rabbits wear pants,
I tiptoe past daisies,
In search of brave fancies.

The sun winks on petals,
While squirrels juggle nettles,
A butterfly sneezed,
And chaos increased!

With a hop and a skip,
I stumble, then trip,
On weeds that conspire,
To raise my attire.

But laughter's the cure,
As I wrangle my shoe,
In this quirky old place,
Where joy finds its pace!

## **Beneath the Canopy**

Beneath leafy covers,
The strange and the wonders,
A hedgehog's in song,
With a voice that is wrong.

Mushrooms wear tiny hats,
While snails sip on fats,
A caterpillar's plight,
Is finding the light!

Parrots are gossiping,
While bees keep on buzzing,
Amidst the sweet smell,
Of chaos, oh well!

With laughter on lips,
And a few playful trips,
In this jungle of cheer,
Silliness is near!

## **Journey into Eden**

A whimsical path leads me,
Where odd critters agree,
To host an odd party,
With fruits nice and hearty.

The monkeys throw pies,
As I dodge and I rise,
A dog in a cape,
Has come to escape!

With laughter erupting,
And fruit flies disrupting,
We spin in a dance,
In this wild happenstance!

So pass me the cake,
And watch squeaky fate,
Where giggles resound,
In this joy I have found!

## Where Wildflowers Dream

In fields where dreams wander,
And silly thoughts ponder,
A daisies charade,
In a flower parade.

A chatty old tree,
Keeps sharing its glee,
While ants play charades,
In slipshod broadsides.

The breeze starts to tickle,
With flowers that giggle,
My socks pull a prank,
And fall in the tank!

With laughter so loud,
I join in the crowd,
In this whimsical dream,
Where wildflowers beam!

**Paths Carved by Nature's Hand**

In a world where weeds play tag,
Roses giggle, the garden's brag.
Shrubs compete in silly dance,
While daisies plot their flower chance.

Butterflies wear ties so bright,
While ants march in a formal flight.
A snail wins the slowest race,
While clovers cheer with leafy grace.

The sun plays peekaboo with clouds,
And pollen swirls in festive crowds.
A bumblebee takes a short nap,
As blooms all plot their funny trap.

So grab your hat, join the fun,
Nature's laughter has just begun.
On nature's paths, with quirky glee,
Life's a joke— come laugh with me!

# The Quiet Festival of Blooming Moments.

Petunias host a costume ball,
While fragrant jasmine sings enthrall.
Tulips serve the punch and cake,
As bees arrive for goodness' sake.

Daisies crown a jolly king,
They dance and spin, all laugh and sing.
A carrot inputs veggie jokes,
As sunflowers giggle with the folks.

The butterfly band plays a tune,
In harmony with the bright moon.
With every bloom, a whisper shared,
In this garden where all cared.

From seedlings small to shrubs so grand,
It's a festival, all hand in hand.
Nature's guests— lighthearted and free,
Celebrate this garden jubilee!

## Whispers at the Arbor

Underneath this leafy dome,
Whispers float and find a home.
Squirrels gossip 'bout the nuts,
While flowers share their latest ruts.

A bud jokes with a weary vine,
Says, "Let's look fine, we must align!"
A cricket chirps with so much zest,
While ladybugs take a fun rest.

The old oak shakes its wrinkled bark,
Revealing tales from dawn till dark.
Its branches sway in laughter's tune,
Beneath the smiling, watchful moon.

Oh, the secrets that trees know,
Of garden antics in the glow.
So let's gather round, share a cheer,
For whispers here are loud and clear!

## Secrets of the Bloom

In the backyard, giggles hum,
Petals sneer at what's become.
"What's that?" asks a flower shy,
"Oh, just seeds that jump and fly!"

Pansies play a card game round,
While violets make the silliest sound.
The sun peeks in, a cheeky face,
Catching garden shenanigans at pace.

Roses blush with jokes so sweet,
While zinnias tap their dancing feet.
A snapshot taken with a worm,
Who's sporting quite a funny term.

Every bloom holds a laughing spell,
In nature's garden, all is well.
These funny secrets wrapped in shade,
Turn the bloom into a merry parade!

## Corners of Light and Leaf

In corners bright, where shadows play,
A squirrel steals a nut and runs away.
The flowers giggle as bees zoom past,
While butterflies dance, oh what a blast!

A gnome grins wide, his hat askew,
Telling tales of frost and morning dew.
With a cheeky wink, he plants a seed,
And waits for laughter, that's all he needs!

A cat chases rays on a sunlit patch,
With every leap, another silly catch.
The sunlight flickers, a playful tease,
As shadows hide behind blooming trees.

With critters bantering in this delight,
Every turn brings giggles, day or night.
In leafy corners where dreams take flight,
Life curtails worries, all feels so right.

## The Painted Gate of Solitude

A gate of colors, bold and bright,
Now welcomes every whimsy in sight.
With polka dots and stripes that swirl,
It spins in laughter, like a joyful whirl.

Behind the gate, a rabbit's scheme,
Turns into an ever-hilarious dream.
He juggles carrots under the moon,
While fireflies hum him a funny tune.

A hedgehog dons a tiny, red bow,
As he struts around, putting on a show.
A chorus of crickets joins the fun,
Creating a concert under the sun.

With each shy whisper and playful glance,
The gate spins stories, inviting a dance.
In solitude's charm, together we stand,
Laughing at life, oh isn't it grand?

## Reveries in the Orchard's Heart

In the orchard's grip, where whimsy thrives,
An apple sings as the laughter dives.
With cheeky smirks and a bounce in its peel,
They all gather 'round to share the appeal.

A wallaby hops, its pouch full of pies,
While owls tell jokes in amusing disguise.
Each branch shakes laughter, a ticklish spree,
While cherries giggle in false reverie.

Around the trunk, a dance begins,
With limber limbs and joyous spins.
While oranges cheer with a zestful glee,
Coaxing the stars for yet more company.

Oh, this orchard bright, such a silly place,
Where every moment's a joyful embrace.
With fruits and critters all playing their part,
Life's sweetest echoes sing from its heart.

## **The Breeze That Knows My Name**

A breeze blows softly, a mischievous friend,
Tickling leaves, it laughs without end.
Whispering secrets, it knows my plight,
Yet tugs on my hat, chasing me light.

A gust that blows hats from heads so proud,
Swirling and twirling, it draws a crowd.
With flowers befriending in playful chatter,
It spins tall tales, oh, nothing else matters!

It teases the cats as they nap on a ledge,
While tickling toes at the garden's edge.
With every flap, it pulls at my clothes,
As I dance with the wind, in laughter it flows.

This breeze that knows my name, I'm quite sure,
Is a prankster, a sprite, a playful lure.
In its delightful wake, giggles unfold,
With stories of summers that never grow old.

## The Serpent's Path

In the grass a snake did slither,
It chuckled softly, oh what a lither!
I asked it for a sign of fate,
It winked and said, "Just dodge the mate!"

With scales that sparkled in the sun,
It coiled around and said, "Let's run!"
We raced the bumblebees in flight,
Laughing as we danced in delight!

Underneath the hedges we did hide,
The gardener's dog looked on with pride.
We threw a party with a card and cake,
But all we had was a slice of snake!

Now if you wander down that lane,
You might just hear a giggling strain.
For in the grass, a tale is spun,
Of a slithering friend and the silly fun!

## A Dance of Shadows

Underneath the moon so bright,
Shadows waltzed in the pale moonlight.
One had two left feet, oh dear,
It tripped on roots, but gave a cheer!

They twisted 'round the garden fence,
A tango that made no sense.
The roses laughed, the daisies swayed,
As shadows danced, their feet arrayed.

A shadow duck fell on its face,
Another joined to win the race.
They spun and twirled with childish glee,
Who knew shadows could be so free?

So if you peek when night is near,
You might just catch this merry cheer.
In a garden filled with light,
The shadows dance till morning bright!

## The Lotus Awakens

In a pond where lilies float,
A lotus stretched its leafy coat.
It yawned, it sighed, it blinked its eyes,
"Is breakfast served?" it asked, surprised.

Frog nearby croaked out a tune,
"Breakfast? Buddy, it's still noon!"
The lotus giggled at this jest,
"I'll just bask, it's quite the quest!"

Water bugs skated, quick as light,
The lotus waved, "Whoa, what a sight!"
"Hold still, my friends, I need to pose,
For selfies under the sun's glow!"

So if you wander near that spree,
You'll find a plant with glee, you see.
For in that pond, with joy it shouts,
"Life's a laugh, that's what it's about!"

## Starlit Blossoms

In a garden where the stars play,
Blossoms giggle and sway all day.
"Oh look, a comet!" one bloom cried,
But it was just a sleepy fly, wide-eyed.

They whispered secrets in the night,
Hiding from the moon's bright light.
"Let's have a party, who's in line?"
"No nectar left, but that's just fine!"

Petals twinkled, colors flashed,
As fireflies in laughter dashed.
In the midst of glee and fun,
They knew they would never be outdone.

So if you hear that fleeting sound,
Of blossoms laughing all around,
Join in their frolic, take a chance,
For in this garden, they all dance!

## **Secrets Beneath the Boughs**

A squirrel wears a tiny hat,
He dances 'round with a chatty rat.
A hedgehog pulls a prank or two,
While rabbits giggle in the dew.

The pastures echo with silly song,
A frog in boots croaks all day long.
The daisies sway, they know the score,
As butterflies argue over the floor.

A cat on a fence practices a pose,
While the sneaky crow steals a rose.
The garden knows secrets and tales,
Of walking shoes and wagging tails.

The moonlight beams on this jolly spree,
Where even the weeds like to tease and be.
A treasure waits where laughter flows,
In a world of mischief where madness grows.

## The Twilight Grove

At dusk, the trees hold a slow dance,
Grasshoppers chirp in a silly trance.
A raccoon slips on his bright tutu,
While ladybugs waltz in a fancy shoe.

The shadows play tricks, hide and seek,
A babbling brook begins to speak.
A poet's pen doodles in the air,
And crickets are staging a Broadway fair.

The owls clap wings, a feathered cheer,
As fireflies light up the jovial sphere.
"Why so serious?" a rabbit shouts,
In a party of veggies, all dancing about!

In the twilight grove, joy swells and swoops,
The only rule? To join in the whoops!
With giggles and grins, the stars take their place,
In this funny night, there's no room for grace.

## Mosaic of Green

In a patchwork quilt of greens and gold,
The garden spins tales, cheeky and bold.
A line of ants with a snack on their back,
Marching to concerts, while crickets attack.

A sunflower yawns, stretching so wide,
While shadows of bushes play peek-a-hide.
A chubby snail takes a ride on a leaf,
Comically slow, bringing everyone grief.

The violets gossip, spilling the tea,
On the buzzing bee who thinks he's a key.
"Let's dance!" the weeds cry, "Join the parade!"
In this happy mix, no one's afraid.

A chortle from daisies, their heads in a spin,
The more, the merrier, let's laugh and grin!
In this mosaic of green and delight,
Every corner glimmers with joy in the night.

## A Palette of Nature

A painter dreams of colors bright,
With flowers posing left and right.
A rainbow stretches, giggles and sighs,
As squirrels giggle, crafting their ties.

Dandelions burst out with silly flair,
While bees in bowties buzz everywhere.
A chicken wearing spectacles crows,
In this riot of hues, anything goes!

A patch of marigolds throws a fit,
When daisies claim they're the most "lit."
Each petal jostles for the best view,
And grasshoppers break into a wild shoe.

With splashes of laughter and strokes of glee,
This palette of nature is wild and free.
Painted in jest, with joy as the theme,
In this quirky garden, life's just a dream.

## Fables Etched in Leafy Shadows

In the garden, whispers tell,
Of flowers that can sing so well.
A rabbit wears a little vest,
He nods and grins, he knows he's blessed.

A fox once tried to dance a jig,
But tripped on roots, oh what a gig!
The daisies laughed, the blooms turned red,
A comedy beneath the spread.

The hedgehog hums a happy tune,
While picking berries, under moon.
He spins and twirls, then takes a bow,
For laughter's worth, he'll show you how.

In shady spots, the turtles race,
They're slow on feet but quick in pace.
The garden's quirks, they know just right,
In leafy realms, they share delight.

## The Tranquil Passage of Time

Amidst the petals, time does skip,
With bumblebees on honey's trip.
A snail insists he's fast as light,
While butterflies take graceful flight.

A wise old owl, he gives survival tips,
To ants who march in synchronized trips.
"Just move like leaves upon the breeze,
And always bring some crumbs, if you please!"

The tortoise boasts of ages vast,
His shell, a throne, his shadow cast.
But youth prevails; they cheer and sway,
In blooms that dance throughout the day.

Giggles echo as daisies bloom,
Each petal holds a little room.
For laughter lives where sunbeams play,
In whims of time, they drift away.

## Where Blossoms Meet the Sky

Up among the blooms that soar,
A squirrel plots to start a war!
With acorns aimed, he shouts, "Let's invade!"
While flowers pout, in shades displayed.

The jolly sun takes off his cap,
As clouds, they giggle in the lap.
A rainbow launches into view,
While frogs in coats say, "That'll do!"

Busy bees don crowns of gold,
While ants play cards, a sight to behold.
The petals rustle, oh what fun,
Games are played 'til day is done!

In the heights where laughter climbs,
The garden's pulse beats out sweet chimes.
A circus blooms as laughter flies,
In this patch where blossoms rise.

## **Footsteps in the Wildflower Breeze**

The wind whirls tales of silly feats,
As gnomes argue 'bout the best of sweets.
One wants cookies, the other, pies,
They debate under the laughing skies.

A ladybug claims she can fly,
But lands on grass with a little sigh.
"Guess I'll need a runway wide,"
She laughs at dreams that cannot glide.

Caterpillars stroll, quite regally fine,
Wearing bow ties made of vine.
They tip their hats, a flourish grand,
In flows of green, they make their stand.

With each step taken in the breeze,
Nature's whimsy brings us ease.
In this wild patch of giggles and cheer,
The garden's magic feels so near.

## Lattice of Light

In the maze of vines, I feel quite spry,
A squirrel runs by, it lets out a cry.
The hedgehog's got plans, or so it seems,
Dreaming of biscuits, not sunbeams.

The sun winks down, oh, what a sight,
Worms are wriggling, dancing in fright.
A ladybug giggles on the leaf,
'Don't munch me, dear, I'm barely a beef!'

The blossoms hum tunes in vibrant array,
The bees have a party, all jazzed for the day.
A tongue-tied bumble decides to break dance,
Buzzing around, hoping for a chance.

By the lattice of light, there's laughter in bloom,
Nature's a comedian, the garden's its room.
With a twist of a stem and a thistle's jest,
Life's giggle fest starts, and we're all just blessed.

## The Story of the Willow

Oh, the willowy lady sways with ease,
Telling tall tales to the summer breeze.
Her branches brush secrets on playful toes,
While gossiping butterflies swoosh as they go.

'Listen close, dear inchworm, I've seen it all,'
Said she with a wave, as the petals do sprawl.
'I've caught the sun's laughter and gentle sighs,
Even the raccoon's late-night pie-crust spies.'

A squirrel drops in with a nutty complaint,
'Why must the birds start their songs like a paint?'
While ants march in line, with crumbs on their backs,
Plotting a feast from the fallen snacks.

So under her shade, all gather near,
Creating a chorus of giggles and cheer.
The willow, like a witty old friend,
Spins tales of delight that never will end.

## **Glimmers Among the Dahlia**

Among the dahlias, in hues so bright,
A gnome loses balance, it's quite a sight!
He tumbles and rolls, caught in the giggle,
As ladybugs shout, 'Hey! Do a jiggle!'

The petals are prim, yet they dance so sly,
While bugs form a band with a passionate cry.
The grasshoppers hop, don their fanciest shoes,
In search of a party with tunes to amuse.

A moth plays the spoons, quite proud of his skill,
With a flower child singing, it's quite the thrill.
The wind claps along, the stars start to peek,
In a dahlia disco, it's fun at its peak.

So come take a stroll through this floral spree,
Where laughter and quirkiness grow like a tree.
In the land of the dahlias, joy's in the air,
Life's a weird garden, no worries, just care.

## The Breath of Spring

Spring's breath is ticklish, it teases the nose,
While bunnies make mischief, wearing big bows.
They hop and they scoot with a whimsical flair,
And quite often trip on their own fluffy hair.

The blooms start to giggle, all colors collide,
As crocuses peek from their wintertime hide.
A crow caws a joke that is shockingly bad,
And the daisies laugh loud, both happy and mad.

With each buzzing bee, there's a song in the air,
The frogs join the chorus, it's positively rare.
A dancing lament from the shy little fern,
Swaying with glee, waiting for its turn.

So raise up a cheer for this season so bright,
With all of its mischief and moments of light.
As spring's breath continues, so carefree, so spry,
Let laughter ring true, as the days flutter by.

## In the Realm of Ivy

In the realm where ivy creeps,
Silly frogs in fancy leaps.
Gnome with a hat too big for him,
Wobbles 'round on a path so slim.

Bees in tuxedos bust a move,
Jive to flowers in a silly groove.
Ladybugs gossip, sipping tea,
Critics of the garden's comedy.

Cats in sunbeams strut like stars,
With low riding pants and fake guitars.
A snail sings sweetly on a leaf,
While worms hold on for dear relief.

Under the arch of petals bright,
Laughter echoes with pure delight.
In this green kingdom so absurd,
Funny antics are simply preferred.

## Serenade by the Sunflower

Sunflowers laugh with their big bright face,
Tickling bees in a dancing race.
A sunflower sways, calls out with glee,
"Come have a chat! There's nectar for free!"

Bumblebees wear bowties quite fine,
While ants march like they own the line.
Crickets recite poems on stems,
As petals spin in humorous hems.

The breeze whispers jokes through the leaves,
Telling tales only the garden believes.
As shadows twist with goofy grace,
All join in, a symphonic embrace.

At sundown, they hold a grand ball,
With critters waltzing—oh, it's a ball!
In this patch where silliness sways,
Joy ignites in funny displays.

## Chasing Butterflies

Butterflies wear jester hats,
Frolicking high, chasing silly spats.
One trips over a daisy's dew,
And giggles float in colors anew.

Kites made of petals sway unreal,
As creatures laugh, sharing a meal.
A toad croaks out in perfect mime,
While chasing dreams with leaps in rhyme.

Children whirl with glee and laughter,
In pursuit of wings, forever after.
With every flutter and sly escape,
They invent games in a world shaped like grapes.

The morning brings a playful cheer,
As whispers of whimsy float near.
In fields of joy, they twirl and spin,
In chasing butterflies, they all win.

## The Charm of Twining Branches

Twining branches twist and play,
Like tangled hair on a sunny day.
Squirrels scurry, flip and flop,
Taking bets on who'll take the drop.

A parrot squawks a cheeky tune,
Swaying about like a silly balloon.
Vines serve tea to lizards so sly,
While flowers giggle, waving goodbye.

Gnomes build towers out of sticks,
While spiders spin their laughing tricks.
Sunlight dapples with a wink and nudge,
As splashes of color won't budge.

In this realm where jokers twine,
Nature's jesters sip from the divine.
Life blooms in joy, with playful prance,
In every branch, there's a funny chance.

## Rustling Leaves and Dreams

In the hush of the leafy breeze,
A squirrel plots his next big tease.
He steals a hat from a sleeping gnome,
And scurries off to plot his dome.

The rabbits join in with a giggle,
As they dance along, doing a wiggle.
They tiptoe near a blooming flower,
And pretend it's a grand magic tower.

A turtle enters with a loud flip,
Wearing sunglasses, he's quite the trip.
He challenges the wind to a race,
But ends up laughing, just keeping pace.

In this garden of whimsy, life's a jest,
Where all the critters come to rest.
They frolic and tumble beneath the sun,
In a world where silliness is just plain fun.

## The Flora Maze

Navigating petals with utmost flair,
Wandering, wondering, without a care.
A bee buzzes by, doing a jig,
While a ladybug joins in, oh so big!

They tumble through daisies with goofy grace,
Declaring this garden their ultimate space.
But a stubborn weed puts up a fight,
Declaring a debate that's heard till night.

Amidst the blooms, chaos reigns supreme,
With flowers that giggle, what a wild dream!
They plot and they plan, oh what a sight,
A floral festival springing to life!

Enjoying the laughter that fills every nook,
The plants share secrets like an open book.
In this maze of green, joy finds its way,
As laughter and blossoms begin to play.

## Beyond the Threshold

Open the door to a world so bright,
Where shadows play tag in the soft twilight.
A cat in a bow tie takes a long stroll,
Stopping to dip in a sunbeam's bowl.

The daisies gossip in their flowery dress,
As dandelions flaunt their feathery mess.
A frog leaps high, then loses his hat,
Slipping on lilies, he falls with a splat!

A parrot bellows jokes from high up a tree,
While the worms in the dirt chuckle with glee.
They host a comedy show with no end,
In this wild garden where giggles blend.

As night falls softly, the moon winks sly,
And whispers sweet secrets to the sleepy sky.
In this whimsical world, laughter is grand,
Where life's simple joys take a delightful stand.

## Evening's Dappled Light

In the golden glow of fading day,
The garden comes alive, ready to play.
A hedgehog in glasses reads an old book,
While fireflies gather for a playful look.

A chubby toad sings a croaky tune,
As crickets keep rhythm 'neath the plump moon.
They throw a party, wild and free,
In honor of all things silly and glee.

The flowers sway with a playful delight,
Joining the fun in the soft twilight.
A raccoon sneaks in, with snacks galore,
Stealing sandwiches from the party floor!

As laughter rings out in the dusky night,
A butterfly twirls in a dazzling flight.
In the heart of the garden, where joy blooms bright,
Evening's dappled light feels perfectly right.

## The Call of the Daisies


Daisies dance in a sunny row,
They tickle the toes of the breezy flow.
A ladybug giggles as it rides by,
On a big sunflower, oh my, oh my!

Bees buzzing round like they're on a spree,
Pollinating flowers, as happy as can be.
But one little bee lost his way in the fray,
Now he's stuck in a daisy, can't find the way!

The butterflies argue who is the best,
With wings that shimmer, they never get rest.
One flutters past with a flamboyant flair,
While another claims, "Do you see my hair?"

So let's grab a laugh from the garden today,
Where daisies and bugs like to frolic and play.
In this patch of laughter, we'll bloom with delight,
And share silly tales until far into night.

## **Meandering Mornings**

The sun peeks in, with a yawn and a stretch,
Morning's a canvas, oh what a sketch!
A squirrel does somersaults, chasing his tail,
While I sip my tea, thinking 'What a tale!'

Birds start their chatter, a riotous crew,
One got a job as a morning DJ too!
"Wake up, everyone!" they croon with glee,
Their tunes are so silly, they rattle the tree.

As I wander through blooms, a snail rolls by slow,
"Ship of the garden!" is what I bestow.
He chuckles in silence, quite proud of his glide,
Check out my shell—homegrown and dyed!

Oh, meandering mornings, a whimsical sight,
With laughter and giggles from dawn until night.
Nature's oddities wrap me in grace,
In this charming chaos, I've found my place.

## Whispers of the Wild

In the thicket, secrets stir with a wink,
A raccoon steals snacks, he's quick as a link.
"Hey, no fair!" cries the owl, wide-eyed and wise,
"A dinner of twigs, is that your big prize?"

Frogs are croaking, they throw quite a fit,
In harmony's whispers, they sing just for grit.
Each ribbit's a joke, each splash is a cheer,
In the chorus of wild, there's nothing to fear.

A fox in a top hat strolls by with flair,
"Evening, my friends! Have you heard of the fair?"
He boasts of his tricks and matching pink shoes,
While hedgehogs giggle in their prickly blues.

Oh, whispers of wild, in the underbush sway,
Bring giggles and folly, come laugh here and play.
In the spotlight of moonlight, mischief awaits,
Join in the ruckus, let's open the gates!

## In the Heart of the Rose

Roses burst forth in a radiant tease,
With petals that blush, they swayed in the breeze.
"Watch your step!" warns a bloom with a grin,
"Don't trample my friends, or you'll start a din!"

Thorns play peekaboo, poking with glee,
Their jokes are quite prickly, just wait and see!
A bee buzzes past, quite lost in the jest,
He lands on a rose that's wearing a vest.

"Just a quick stop for pollen," he shouts,
Yet fumbles and slips as the petals twist out.
The flowers erupt in a radiant chuckle,
While the humble little bee flutters and snuggles.

So welcome the laughter that blooms in the air,
In the heart of the rose, there's joy to share.
A patch of pure whimsy, where funny takes flight,
In the garden of giggles, everything's right!

## The Whispering Orchard

The apples chatter, green and red,
They gossip low, about your head.
The pears roll laughs, in twirling stance,
While cherries plot a funny dance.

A squirrel pranks a grumpy bee,
He sneaks up close—oh, can't you see?
The blossoms giggle, blush, then sway,
As freckled sunbeams play their play.

In this wild feast of fruity fun,
Each fruit a jester, just begun.
If laughter's fruit, then take a bite,
In this orchard, all feels right.

So tiptoe softly, hear the jest,
In every branch, a playful quest.
Where every laugh is ripe and sweet,
Join the fruit in their playful beat.

## Dreaming among the Lilies

The lilies wear their best attire,
With polka dots of bright desire.
They sway and spin, like kids at play,
Playing hopscotch 'round the bay.

A frog joins in with leaps so bold,
In muddy leaps, he feels quite gold.
The bugs are busy in a line,
Trading secrets, sipping wine.

With petals soft, they pull a prank,
A dance-off sparks near the riverbank.
As crickets laugh and join the song,
In floral dreams, we all belong.

Among the blooms, laughter ensues,
In colorful whispers, joy infused.
So leap and twirl where comedy reigns,
In the kingdom where silliness reigns.

## **A Constellation of Petals**

Starlit petals light the way,
As daisies giggle, come what may.
Tulips wear quirky hats on high,
In this garden, you can't deny.

The roses sigh in mock despair,
With thorns that tickle, quite unfair.
They trade their secrets, loud and clear,
"Did you hear? The sun's not here!"

With lilies laughing, oh so spry,
They scheme to make the bees all fly.
With every bloom, a chuckle flows,
In this cosmos where humor grows.

So pluck a laugh, and toss it wide,
In a sprinkle where joy can glide.
Amongst this riot of colors bright,
Find fun in petals, pure delight.

## The Pulse of the Meadow

In the meadow pulse, a funny scene,
Where daisies play, the grass is green.
A butterfly's a giggling fool,
He flutters by to break the rule.

The dandelions chat, quite proud,
With whispers soft, they cheer aloud.
"Let's blow some seeds and start a spree!"
"Oh yes, but not too close to me!"

A clumsy bumblebee just sneezed,
With pollen clouds, he looks quite pleased.
While tumbleweeds roll on the run,
Chasing laughter, just for fun.

So dance among the sprightly tune,
Where laughter blooms beneath the moon.
With every step, the grass will sway,
In this meadow, come and play!

## Lanterns of Nightshade Dreams

In moonlight's glow, the shadows dance,
A toad serenades, lost in a trance.
The daisies giggle, the roses tease,
While squirrels debate the best way to sneeze.

A rabbit in boots, with a top hat so tall,
Claims he can juggle, then fumbles and falls.
The fireflies blink like a disco ball,
Inviting all critters to join in the ball.

The hedgehogs wear goggles, they zoom on their bikes,
While chipmunks hold races on miniature spikes.
Laughter erupts as the wildflowers sway,
From creatures who think it's a holiday play.

In the world of whimsy, where fun meets the night,
Every wrong turn feels deliciously right.
So join in the chaos, just follow the gleam,
In the garden of dreams, we wake up the dream.

## A Tapestry of Petal Dreams

Petals are pinwheels on a breezy spree,
They twirl and they giggle, as bright as can be.
Butterflies whisper, 'What's the next theme?'
While spiders knit webs that sparkle and beam.

A cat in a waistcoat recites a grand rhyme,
Completely forgetting the passage of time.
He pauses for snacks, a feast for his whiskers,
As ladybugs chuckle and share garden whispers.

Sunflowers stand tall, playing king for a day,
While the daisies quip, "We just bloom their way!"
The bees pull a prank, with a giggling buzz,
The ants stage a coup, as they plot to take fuzz.

Amidst the bloom, all trouble seems sweet,
In this tapestry spun from joy and from heat.
So laugh with the blossoms, let whimsy take flight,
In a garden where dreams light the canvas of night.

## Secrets Woven in Greenery

In tangled vines, secrets twine,
A raccoon's plotting, with a mischievous line.
The ferns hold their breath, keen to confide,
What happens when hedgehogs take joyrides.

The cats play chess with a couple of mice,
The mice brandish cheese, oh, ain't that nice!
A tree stands aloof, watching it all,
As critters collide with no worry or brawl.

Fireflies are gossiping, buzzing about,
Planning a party, with laughter, no doubt.
The owls roll their eyes, with tales far and wide,
While flowers discuss how to best bend and glide.

In this leafy realm, where the silly reside,
Secrets grow louder, there's nowhere to hide.
So jive with the plants, embrace every scheme,
As we spin through the verdant and whimsical dream.

## The Glistening Path to Wonder

Down the glimmering path where giggles await,
A mole in a monocle surveys the great state.
With mushrooms as umbrellas, they dance in the rain,
And frogs in tuxedos sing sweetly in vain.

A tangible joy sprouts with each silly step,
While daisies kick back, moonwalking the prep.
The shadows unfold with a smirk and a wink,
Inviting all creatures to pause and to think.

Grasshoppers leap with a flair quite surreal,
While turtles debate what's the best kind of meal.
The air is filled with tales of enchantment,
Where laughter is woven with carefree merriment.

So join in the jaunt on a path paved with cheer,
Where every small critter is welcome and near.
In the dance of the night, with wonder in sight,
A glistening journey through joyous delight.

## The Nectar of Time

Beneath the sun, I dance with bees,
Trying to sip on the sweetest tease.
A flower giggles when I arrive,
"I'm not honey, but let's still vibe!"

The clock ticks loud in this bloom-filled sphere,
While daisies debate the best time for cheer.
One says noon, while another claims night,
"Let's settle this over some bug soup tonight!"

Petals whisper secrets of ages gone past,
As clumsy butterflies uncover spells cast.
The grass snickers, a riotous sound,
At the way I trip, tumbling around!

In every corner, a riddle in sight,
I chuckle at daisies that boast of their height.
"Hey, little buddy, stay humble, stay prime,
We're all just here, sharing this nectar of time!"

## In the Embrace of Ferns

Ferns in a hug, so plush and so bright,
They swish and sway, oh what a sight!
"Join the party!" they call with glee,
But I can't dance; I'm stuck in a tree!

Their fronds flutter like big, leafy arms,
Inviting all critters to share in their charms.
A squirrel pop-corns while the rabbit sprints,
"Hey you, feather-duster, stop with the hints!"

Residing beneath this leafy green roof,
The ladybugs claim, "We do just poof!"
With laughter that bounces from stem to their toes,
Each mistake is a victory, as everyone knows!

So we giggle and wiggle with wild, carefree airs,
Among all the ferns, we shed our cares.
Let's beam in the shade, holding the light,
In the embrace of ferns, everything feels right!

## **Lullabies of the Meadow**


A meadow sings, with voices so fine,
Grasshoppers chirp in a rhythm divine.
The daisies hum after a long summer day,
While dandelions shout, "Come, join our play!"

Frogs croak a tune as the sun bids adieu,
Each rhythm a giggle, each beat a woohoo.
The clouds roll in; they puff up and swirl,
While the moon winks down, launching a twirl!

Crickets take lead with a strum and a beat,
While fireflies flash in a dance full of heat.
"Tonight we shall glow!" the mushrooms declare,
"Let's leave the dampness behind and not care!"

As stars twinkle softly, dreams dance along,
The meadows are waking, with laughter and song.
So let's rest our heads where the green grasses sway,
And enjoy the lullabies till break of the day!

## A Maze in Full Bloom

In a labyrinth of petals, I peek around,
I find myself lost, with giggles abound.
The roses all jest, "You were so sure,
But look at you now, can you find the door?"

Tulips tease softly, sharing a plot,
"Oh look, here's a path, well maybe, it's not."
With each twist and turn, I trip and I sway,
All the flowers cheer, "You're doing okay!"

A bumblebee chuckles, buzzing all near,
"Don't fret; I've been lost, let's share a cold beer!"
With petals of laughter and scents of delight,
We search for the exit, still giggling at night.

At last, I find blooms that signal the way,
The sunflowers grin, "You made it! Hooray!"
In the maze of blossoms, whirling so wild,
Every corner brings laughter, making me feel like a child!

## **Whispers of Blooming Paths**

In the maze of daisies, all lost and found,
A squirrel's doing ballet, I can't believe my eyes.
Tulips gossip loudly, their colors astound,
While dandelions hold court, dispensing weird lies.

A bee with a bowtie sips tea on a leaf,
Telling tales of a snail with a newfound speed.
Sunflowers chuckle, 'What a silly belief!'
As ladybugs roll dice, counting all of their seeds.

With socks on my feet, I'm chasing a cat,
Who thinks this whole journey's a marvelous game.
While worms gather round for a chat and a pat,
Each flower's a muse, but they all look the same.

So I tiptoe around, trying not to offend,
The petals that giggle, the vines that have sass.
In this garden of whims, I'm seeking a friend,
But the frogs just keep croaking; let's all raise a glass!

## The Secret Doorway to Eden

Behind the green hedges, where secrets are sweet,
A rabbit named Rufus discusses his dreams.
He just wants some lettuce and comfy warm seats,
While the roses debate the best chocolate creams.

A hedgehog with glasses is busy on tax,
Confused by the numbers that just don't make sense.
The violets are giggling, they've been known to relax,
As bees have a dance-off, showing off their immense!

With bouncy old gnomes trying hard to keep pace,
Their hats fly like kites in the breeze of delight.
Each shrub's bursting laughter; you can't miss the face,
Of a bloom with a bowtie who's dressed for the night.

So come join the circus of petals and bugs,
Where squirrels juggle acorns and sun shines like gold.
In this secret haven of laughter and hugs,
Even weeds have their moments, or so I've been told!

## Beyond the Arbor's Embrace

Under arches of ivy, a squirrel in a hat,
Proclaims it's a party; the daisies agree.
The tulips are jiving, what do you think of that?
While ferns stand around, sipping lemonade tea.

A cat in a bowtie recites Shakespeare loud,
While caterpillars clap with a dazzling cheer.
The roses form circles, all laughing, so proud,
As butterflies flit and bring joy to the sphere.

Let's tango with petals, let's waltz with the ants,
We'll boogie with blossoms, let's make a new trend.
As drip-drop the raindrops lend dance to the plants,
We'll frolic and tumble, and never pretend!

So swing by the gate, bring your quirkiest grin,
For this garden of wonders is bursting with glee.
With friends all around, let the fun times begin,
In this world of wild blooms, come play and be free!

## Wandering in Flora's Realm

Strolling through colors, my heart feels so light,
A mannequin lily dances with flair.
Giggling geraniums, oh what a sight!
While peonies whisper, 'We just love to share!'

A gnome's out here juggling some fruit in a tub,
While the ferns gossip over a cup of fine tea.
A snail took a selfie—what an adorable shrub!
As daisies debate who's the fairest of three.

So roving with pollen, I skip here and there,
The daisies are disco-ing; come join the parade!
With a twirl and a leap, we will kick off the air,
As laughter erupts where the blooms have been laid.

At dusk we will toast with the fireflies' glow,
To the magic of laughter and friendships we've spun.
In this whimsical realm, no melody slow,
Each flower a note in the symphony of fun!

www.ingramcontent.com/pod-product-compliance
Lightning Source LLC
Chambersburg PA
CBHW071853160426
43209CB00003B/534